MAGIC CARPETS

30 EASY-TO-MAKE RUG DESIGNS

MELINDA COSS · SYLVIE SOUDAN

St. Martin's Press
New York

Library of Congress Catalog
Card Number: 88-43643

ISBN 0-312-03027-4

First published in Great Britain
by William Collins Sons & Co.
Ltd, 1989

First U.S. Edition

10 9 8 7 6 5 4 3 2 1

Designer Janet James
Photographer Tif Hunter
Stylist Rebecca Gillies
Line Illustrations Sandra Pond
Executive Editor Cathy Gosling
Editor Caroline White

The authors would like to thank
the management and staff at
Readicut for their assistance in
the production of all the sample
rugs used for photography.

Typeset by Ace Filmsetting Ltd,
Frome, Somerset
Colour reproduction by Bright
Arts (HK) Ltd, Hong Kong
Printed by New Interlitho, SpA,
Italy

CONTENTS

INTRODUCTION

The 1980s have seen a revolution in design consciousness. Glossy magazines everywhere present us with endless choices from which to select textiles and furnishings to reflect our own individual style and personality. Traditional crafts, such as knitting, have risen to the status of high fashion and more and more people are expressing their creativity through craft-based skills. Making something yourself is both an opportunity to create a beautiful, high quality object that can be treasured and passed down from generation to generation, and a practical and rewarding pastime for the whole family.

In *Magic Carpets* we have endeavoured to cover a wide range of traditional and modern rug and carpet designs that are, above all, easy to make. There are 30 rugs, all specially designed for this book: some of them are centrepieces in their own right, others will add richness and dimension to any room, while rugs like the polar bearskin are strictly for fun!

The purpose of the book is to dispel the myth that a complicated design requires endless skill to achieve. The beauty of the latch-hooking method of rugmaking is the fact that only one basic movement is required, plus, of course, the ability to read a chart, which we promise is quite painless! Also, mistakes are easily rectified since each knot can be removed individually. As each tuft is independent of those on either side, the colours used in the design can change with every knot, if so desired. This method therefore naturally lends itself to exceptionally free designs.

We also describe the technique for working your rugs in needlepoint using cross stitch or continental stitch, and you can, in principle, select either of these methods to reproduce our rug designs. We have, however, latch-hooked all but two of the rugs in the book since we found this the easiest method to accomplish the results we wanted. In addition, there are sections on trims and finishes, and instructions on how to design your own rugs.

Once you have made one, or several, of the rugs in this book and have discovered what you are capable of, you will see the infinite possibilities for creating your own exciting rug designs. The rugs can be used traditionally on the floor, hung on the wall, or draped over furniture. Whatever your choice, they will add colour and comfort to your home and you will have the added satisfaction of knowing that you 'made it yourself'.

A BRIEF HISTORY

Rugmaking has its origins in a time, perhaps two thousand years before Christ, when nomadic tribes led their flocks through the bitter winter weather of Central Asia and hunting provided the only means of survival. Fabrics were woven from compressed sheep's wool and used for blankets and floor coverings, thus providing protection and warmth.

As the nomads' skills evolved, vivid and glorious dyes were extracted from the vegetable sources available, such as pomegranates, turmeric berries, oak apples and walnut shells. These were boiled in vats before the immersion of the wool, which was first treated with sheep's dung. A loom of simple oak branches made the creation of a length of woollen cloth possible. The next step was the twisting of short lengths of wool into coloured tufts, leading to the first soft pile, and the patterning that later came to illustrate and identify the lifestyle of particular nomadic tribes.

As these tribes developed into village communities, refined techniques led to the use of cottons and silks in addition to the traditional sheep's wool and goat's hair. Designs, originally drawn from the flowers and trees of the surrounding countryside, were simplified into stylised and abstract patterning. They were intricately knotted by the hands of women and children, many of whom were taught the skill from the age of three years. With carpets becoming a valuable source of barter, whole families worked together, sleeping, living and eating off the huge floor looms that filled their homes.

As towns sprang up throughout the Middle East, merchants encouraged the setting up of workshops where carpets were made at the rate of 1,000 knots per hour. Powerful leaders created court workshops where weavers who demonstrated exceptional talent and craftsmanship created works of art, the beauty of which was considered a reflection of the wealth and prestige of their masters. The use of fine silk required very close clipping to give definition to the intricate patterning and design, and so it was said that 'the thinner the carpet, the richer the Sultan'.

While China adorned its carpets with butterflies, peacocks and dragons, the Islamic religion forbade any portrayal of living creatures. The colour green was never used as this was considered to be 'the colour of the Prophet', and any mistakes on a finished carpet were declared 'deliberate', since nothing should be permitted to rival the perfection of Allah.

Though research into rugmaking suggests origins stemming from the Middle and Far East, very little historic fact has been established as to its precise geographical beginnings. The need for the warmth provided by rugs suggests a universal development amongst primitive tribes, with only the methods of manufacture differing from country to country.

The Anglo-Saxon word 'rug' is of Scandinavian derivation, and in fact hand-hooked rugs, with their rich, fur-like pile, originated with the Vikings who used the thick, weather-resistant fabric for clothing and wall insulation. The arrival of the Vikings in Great Britain in AD 93 spread this technique throughout the country, and in the early seventeenth century the Pilgrims took the skill to America where rags and blankets were cut into strips which were then hooked into hardwearing, colourful rugs and bed coverings. In America today many hand-hooked rugs and carpets have attained artform status.

The 'Latch', or 'Latchet Hook' as it is sometimes known, was developed in England in the mid-1920s. The hook is a combination of a hand hook and a latchet, and was derived from commercial knitting machines. This particular form of rugmaking became popular in the mid-1930s, and is still a firm favourite because of its simplicity and versatility.

LATCH-HOOKED RUGS

Equipment and Materials

A latch-hook (latchet hook): two types of hook are available, both with wooden handles and a steel hook and latchet. The stem of the hook can be curved or straight.
A sharp sewing needle.
Strong thread.

CANVAS

The canvas used for latch-hooking has an open mesh of double threads with approximately three holes to 2.5 cm (1 in). It can be purchased in a variety of widths and is cut to your requested length. This means that whilst the edges on each side are woven and properly finished, you have a raw edge at the top and bottom of your backing. The 'Finishing' section (see p. 10) explains how to deal with these raw edges, but when purchasing your canvas be sure to allow at least an extra four holes at each end for finishing. All the designs in this book are to standard canvas sizes so your design should completely fill all the holes between the two woven edges. It is possible, however, when working on a large rug, to join canvases (see p. 10).

YARN

Rug wool is available by the hank or in ready-cut lengths of approximately 6.5 cm (2½ in).

All the designs in this book are available in kit form, with the correct amount of yarn and a hand-stencilled canvas (see p. 128 for addresses).

Method

There are two different methods of latch-hooking. If only one person is working a rug, either method can be used, but the whole rug should be worked in this one selected method. When two people are working from different ends of the rug, it is important that one uses Method 1 and the other Method 2 in order to keep the pile in the same direction.

The yarn is knotted on the threads of the canvas which run horizontally from woven selvedge to woven selvedge.

NOTE: Whilst it is tempting to work each colour section separately, it is important that you complete one row of knots before starting the next.

FRAMES

Readicut produce a special table on which to work latch-hooked rugs, although it is not strictly essential to use a frame when making a rug by this method.

Method 1

Fold a piece of rug wool in half and place the loop behind the shaft of the hook.

Push the hook down through one hole of the canvas and up through the one directly in front.

Place the two ends of wool round the hook. Pull the hook back through the hole, and loop (closing the latchet).

Pull the two ends of wool gently, tightening the knot.

Latch-hook Method 2

Push the hook under the double thread of canvas past the latchet, and catch the loop of folded wool.

Pull the hook until the loop of wool comes up through the hole.

Push the hook and latchet forwards through the loop of wool and catch the hook round both ends of the held wool.

Pull the hook back, pulling the wool ends through the loop. Pull the wool to tighten the knot (see Method 1, fig. 4).

CROSS-STITCH RUGS

Equipment and Materials

Use a rug or tapestry needle with a blunt point and a hole large enough to accommodate four-ply rug wool or two strands of tapestry wool.

CANVAS

The canvas used in this book has approximately five holes to 2.5 cm (1 in). You can adjust the size of the rug by using finer canvas and yarn, but be sure that you use a strong, coated canvas with a regular mesh.

All the designs in this book are available in kit form, with the correct canvas (see p. 128 for addresses).

FRAMES

In order to keep your tension even it is important that needle-point rugs are worked on a sturdy wooden frame, either a hand-held or free-standing one.

Commercially made frames are readily available; alternatively, it is possible to make an improvised frame by simply gluing together four strips of softwood and bracing the inside corners with metal brackets. A picture frame can be adapted to suit the purpose, or the rug canvas could even be stretched across the base of an old card table and pinned or laced into position.

Do not be tempted to work without a frame, since the rug will become distorted. This may only become evident when you have nearly completed your work.

YARN

We have used four-ply rug wool, which is supplied on hank, although doubled-up tapestry wool or silks can be used. We recommend that you select your yarn on the basis of the amount of wear your rug is likely to receive, since floor use obviously demands a harder-wearing pile. Huge pattern variations are possible by stranding different shades of yarn together.

All the designs in this book are available in kit form, with the correct amount of yarn (see p. 128 for addresses).

TECHNIQUES

Stitches

In this book we have selected cross stitch and continental stitch out of the many possibilities. While the doubled-up effect of cross stitch adds years to the lifespan of your finished rug, continental stitch can be used for speed and will provide a tapestry element to the designs. It might be more suitable if you intend to use your rug as a wall hanging.

CROSS STITCH

Fix the canvas securely in your frame. Start your work at the bottom left-hand corner of the canvas and work in horizontal rows, filling in each block of colour separately.

At the end of each row reverse the working direction and form the new stitch row directly below or above the stitches just completed.

Be sure to keep your tension even throughout the work, as loose tension makes your rug susceptible to snagging, and tension that is too tight will distort your finished work.

CONTINENTAL STITCH

Continental stitch (or half-cross stitch) is often used as a speedy alternative to cross stitch.

Cross stitch

Bring your threaded needle up through square 1 and diagonally down through square 2.

Continue up through square 3 and across to square 4.

When the row is complete, take the needle down and up through the square directly below.

Continue across to square 2, then down and up through square 3, across to square 4 and back up through square 3 again, ready to start your next stitch.

Start your work at the upper right-hand corner of the canvas, leaving a good length of yarn for sewing in on the back of the work.

Bring your needle up through the back of your canvas on the second hole down and the second hole in of your design. Re-insert your needle in the first hole on the first row of your work. Always work from right to left, keeping your tension even.

TECHNIQUES

FINISHING AND USEFUL TIPS

Reading a Chart

With the exception of one of the tartan rugs, the charts in this book are complete representations of the finished designs. With the latch-hooked rugs, every coloured square represents a knot in the finished canvas, and that knot should be made on the horizontal thread that runs *above* each hole; in other words, see each coloured square on your chart as a hole and the top line of the square as the position for the knot.

When working a cross-stitch rug refer to the diagrams on p. 9 for stitch positioning.

Joining Canvas

When joining latch-hook or cross-stitch canvas it is advisable to leave at least five rows of holes for each piece to be overlapped. Place the two blank areas of canvas one on top of the other (lining up the holes) and work knots or stitches through both pieces of the canvas.

Trim away any ends of canvas that show through.

Finishing

When your rug is completely worked the canvas should be cut to shape, leaving an allowance of approximately four holes at the raw edges. Whilst you will already have folded under and hooked through the raw edges on your oblong or square rug, with a shaped rug it is necessary to finish and bind these edges to create a neat, hard-wearing finish. To do this, simply turn the surplus canvas neatly under your finished work and, using strong cotton thread, sew it to the underside of your rug, using one stitch for each hole in the canvas.

On a circular rug you may wish to make a small cut in the canvas before folding it under, to ensure a flat edge. To bind your finished rug simply lay 4-cm (1½-in)-wide cotton binding tape over the raw edge of the canvas and carefully stitch it to the canvas. Sew the tape all the way around your work, making pleats where necessary to take up any excess. The tape should be stitched down at both edges so the raw seam is completely covered.

To finish the woven edges of your canvas simply fold these underneath your finished work and stitch them securely to the backing.

Binding Tape

Binding tape can be purchased from Readicut or, alternatively, buy a heavy-duty cotton tape (approximately 4 cm (1½ in) wide) from any good haberdashery shop.

TECHNIQUES

DESIGNING YOUR OWN RUG

Fringes

Fringes are an attractive way to finish rugs, and they are very simple to make.

Cut your yarn into 30-cm (12-in) lengths and fold two of these lengths in half. Working from left to right, using your latchet hook, pull the looped yarn through the first canvas hole. Pull the four loose ends of yarn through the loop, and pull gently to make a knot.

Repeat this procedure across all the remaining holes, thus forming a row of tassels.

The tassels should then be tied together in the following order. Starting from the left, take the first and third tassels and tie them together using an overhand knot. Pull this knot tight, approximately 2.5 cm (1 in) from the end of the rug. Take the second and fifth tassels and knot these in the same way. Continue in this way knotting the fourth and seventh, then the sixth and ninth, etc., until the row has been completed. Trim the ends to form an even row.

Selecting a Design

Designing your own rug offers a wealth of opportunities for self-expression. Ideas for designs can be taken from post-cards, book illustrations, fabrics and wallpapers, and there are many resource books which will provide inspiration for both traditional and modern patterns.

Firstly, you should determine the size of rug you wish to make and buy suitable canvas for the rugmaking method you intend to use.

If a standard-shaped canvas is all that's required, the simplest approach is to draw your pattern on graph paper, allowing one square per hole of canvas. Using a pencil, roughly sketch your design on to the graph paper. When you are happy with the shape, experiment with colour schemes, using coloured pencils, pastels or watercolour paints. A good guiding principle is to choose a colour scheme to complement the room in which the rug will be placed.

When you have achieved the desired result, carefully outline the areas of colour in black pen, remembering to allow four blank squares at each of the rough edges of the canvas for finishing. Select yarns to match your chosen colours which are suitable for your canvas, and commence working from your chart.

NOTE

For instructions on the latch-hooking technique please refer throughout the rug patterns to pages 7 and 8.

*The designs in this chapter
are a tribute to the rich
and glorious origins of
rugmaking. We have
taken colours and motifs
from traditional sources all
over the world to create
rugs which will look good
in both contemporary and
classic decors.*

PERSIAN
GARDEN

*Worked in a combination
of rich autumn colours,
this rug is an adaptation of
traditional Persian motifs
to a contemporary design.*

PERSIAN GARDEN

Method

Latch-hooking.

Finished Size

152 × 152 cm (60 × 60 in) approximately.

Materials

Piece of latch-hook canvas, 198 × 198 holes between selvedges, plus selvedge allowance.

6.5-cm (2½-in) lengths of rug wool in the following colours:

	lengths
SAPPHIRE	17,640
CHESTNUT	11,560
CHOCOLATE	3,170
GOLD	2,570
BURNT ORANGE	2,500
EMERALD	1,750
STONE	840
CLARET	750
ROSE	620
BUTTER	580

Latch-hook, strong thread, sharp sewing needle.

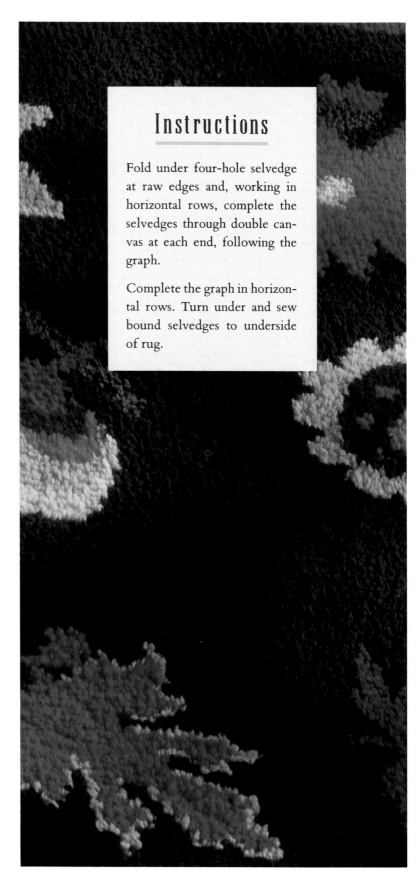

Instructions

Fold under four-hole selvedge at raw edges and, working in horizontal rows, complete the selvedges through double canvas at each end, following the graph.

Complete the graph in horizontal rows. Turn under and sew bound selvedges to underside of rug.

a SAPPHIRE   f EMERALD

b CHESTNUT   g STONE

c CHOCOLATE   h CLARET

d GOLD   i ROSE

e BURNT ORANGE   j BUTTER

ORIENTAL

Flying birds, blossoms and chrysanthemums worked in washed pastels decorate the path of the little trumpeter and the flag boy.

The publishers would like to thank Neal Street East for providing props for use in this photograph.

ORIENTAL

Method

Latch-hooking.

Finished Size

114 × 191 cm (45 × 75 in) approximately.

Materials

Piece of latch-hook canvas, 150 × 252 holes between selvedges, plus selvedge allowance.

6.5-cm (2½-in) lengths of rug wool in the following colours:

		lengths
ECRU		27,350
AQUA		3,320
BUTTER		2,580
LIGHT TURQUOISE		2,160
PALE PINK		1,490
CAMEL		640
LEMON		610
PEACH		550
ICE BLUE		300

Latch-hook, strong thread, sharp sewing needle.

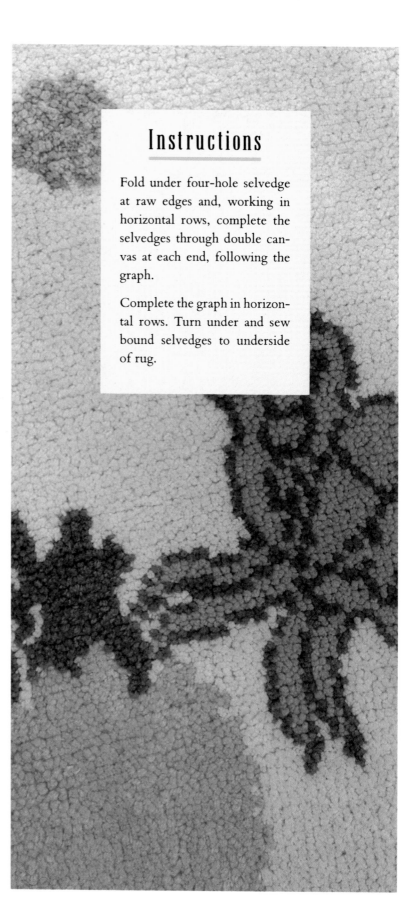

Instructions

Fold under four-hole selvedge at raw edges and, working in horizontal rows, complete the selvedges through double canvas at each end, following the graph.

Complete the graph in horizontal rows. Turn under and sew bound selvedges to underside of rug.

a ECRU

b AQUA

c BUTTER

d LIGHT TURQUOISE

e PALE PINK

f CAMEL

g LEMON

h PEACH

i ICE BLUE

AZTEC

A combination of bold
random stripes and primi-
tive motifs give this rug an
ethnic, woven look like
the beautiful wall-hang-
ings of South America.

AZTEC

Method

Latch-hooking.

Finished Size

152 × 115 cm (60 × 45 in) approximately.

Materials

Piece of latch-hook canvas, 200 × 150 holes between selvedges, plus selvedge allowance.

6.5-cm (2½-in) lengths of rug wool in the following colours:

	lengths
BEIGE	8,640
CHOCOLATE	6,310
COPPER	5,810
AZURE	3,440
MOSS	2,980
ECRU	2,600

5 × 50 g (2 oz) balls of 100% rug wool for fringing.

Latch-hook, strong thread, sharp sewing needle.

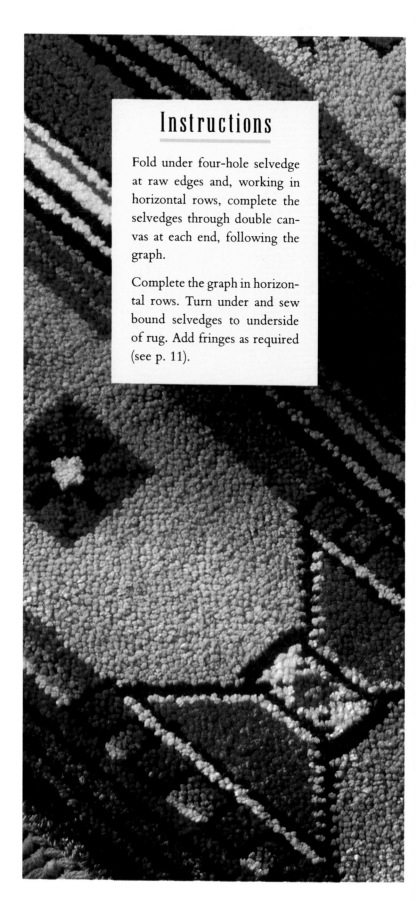

Instructions

Fold under four-hole selvedge at raw edges and, working in horizontal rows, complete the selvedges through double canvas at each end, following the graph.

Complete the graph in horizontal rows. Turn under and sew bound selvedges to underside of rug. Add fringes as required (see p. 11).

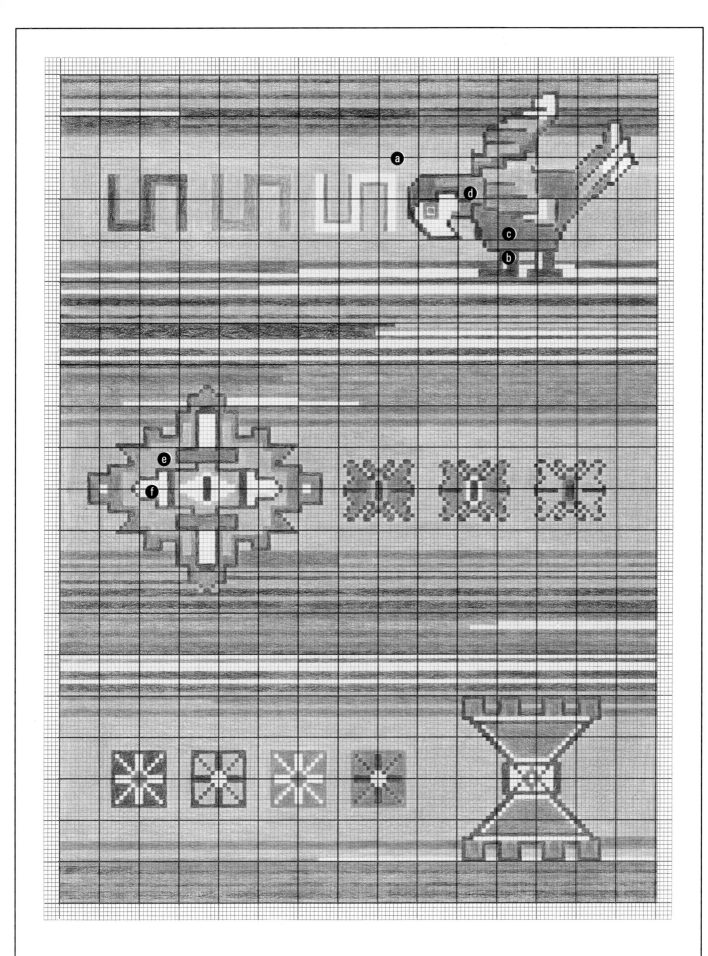

a BEIGE   b CHOCOLATE   c COPPER   d AZURE   e MOSS   f ECRU

INDIAN

This delightful baby elephant chasing a bird was inspired by a temple hanging from Ahmedabad in Gujarat, India. The richness of the colours, combined with the whimsical design, make this rug suitable for many different settings.

INDIAN

Method

Latch-hooking.

Finished Size

92 × 152 cm (36 × 60 in) approximately.

Materials

Piece of latch-hook canvas, 120 × 200 holes between selvedges, plus selvedge allowance.

6.5-cm (2½-in) lengths of rug wool in the following colours:

	lengths
DEEP JADE	17,970
SCARLET	2,880
GOLD	1,270
ECRU	910
AZURE	900
SUNSHINE	320
AQUA	310

Latch-hook, strong thread, sharp sewing needle.

Instructions

Fold under four-hole selvedge at raw edges and, working in horizontal rows, complete the selvedges through double canvas at each end, following the graph.

Complete the graph in horizontal rows. Turn under and sew bound selvedges to underside of rug.

a DEEP JADE

b SCARLET

c GOLD

d ECRU

e AZURE

f SUNSHINE

g AQUA

EGYPTIAN

This rug was inspired by the Egyptian tomb paintings of Deir el-Medina, near the Valley of the Kings. It shows Sennedjem, a royal artisan, and his wife involved in ceremonial harvesting.

EGYPTIAN

Method

Latch-hooking.

Finished Size

115 × 191 cm (45 × 75 in) approximately.

Materials

Piece of latch-hook canvas, 150 × 252 holes between selvedges, plus selvedge allowance.

6.5-cm (2½-in) lengths of rug wool in the following colours:

	lengths
BUTTER	27,190
COPPER	3,650
ECRU	2,180
GRASS	2,150
CAMEL	980
SAPPHIRE	800
BRIGHT RED	750
BLACK	620
GOLD	220

Latch-hook, strong thread, sharp sewing needle.

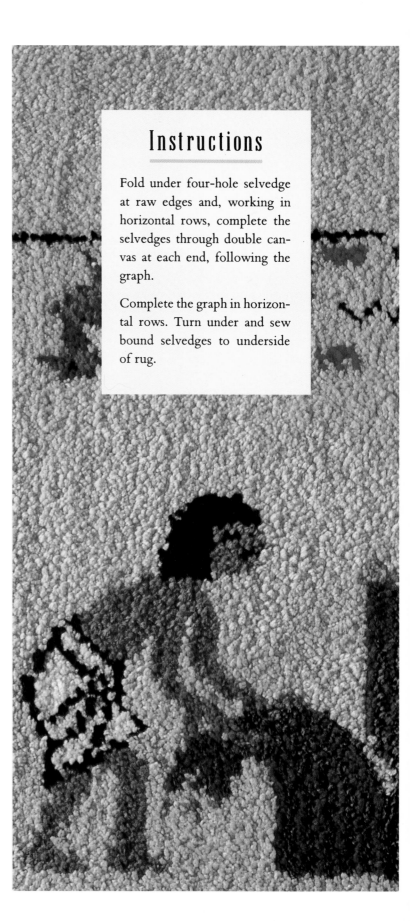

Instructions

Fold under four-hole selvedge at raw edges and, working in horizontal rows, complete the selvedges through double canvas at each end, following the graph.

Complete the graph in horizontal rows. Turn under and sew bound selvedges to underside of rug.

a BUTTER

b COPPER

c ECRU

d GRASS

e CAMEL

f SAPPHIRE

g BRIGHT RED

h BLACK

i GOLD

HIGHLAND
FLING

*A choice of two traditional
tartan rugs in contrasting
colours, which will look
good in the Highlands or
the Lowlands.*

HIGHLAND FLING

Method

Rug 1 (grey background)
Latch-hooking.

Finished Size

Rug 1
77 × 110 cm (30 × 43 in)
approximately.

Materials

Rug 1
Piece of latch-hook canvas, 99 × 144 holes between selvedges, plus selvedge allowance.

6.5-cm (2½-in) lengths of rug wool in the following colours:

	lengths
SLATE	4,100
BLACK	3,460
AZURE	2,900
SILVER	1,350
FOREST GREEN	1,350
WHITE	1,170

Latch-hook, strong thread, sharp sewing needle.

Instructions

Fold under four-hole selvedge at raw edges and, working in horizontal rows, complete the selvedges through double canvas at each end, following the graph.

Complete the graph in horizontal rows. Turn under and sew bound selvedges to underside of rug.

To make rug 2, work from the bottom row of the graph upwards and then repeat the pattern twice. Add fringes as required (see p. 11).

Method

Rug 2 (green background)
Latch-hooking.

Finished Size

Rug 2
77 × 114 cm (30 × 45 in)
approximately.

Materials

Rug 2
Piece of latch-hook canvas, 99 × 150 holes between selvedges, plus selvedge allowance.

6.5-cm (2½-in) lengths of rug wool in the following colours:

	lengths
SKY BLUE	4,810
BRIGHT RED	4,450
FOREST GREEN	3,640
WHITE	2,010

3 × 50 g (2 oz) balls of 100% rug wool for fringing.

Latch-hook, strong thread, sharp sewing needle.

Rug 1

a SLATE

b BLACK

c AZURE

d SILVER

e FOREST GREEN

f WHITE

Rug 2

a SKY BLUE

b BRIGHT RED

c FOREST GREEN

d WHITE

35

Drawing inspiration from nature, the following designs bring the vivid colours of flora and fauna into your home. Each rug can be used on the floor or as a wall-hanging.

WINDFALL

Bright yellow plums are being blown from the sky in this autumnal design.

WINDFALL

Method

Latch-hooking.

Finished Size

77 × 127 cm (30 × 50 in) approximately.

Materials

Piece of latch-hook canvas, 99 × 167 holes between selvedges, plus selvedge allowance.

6.5-cm (2½-in) lengths of rug wool in the following colours:

	lengths
SUNSHINE	4,800
SKY BLUE	4,120
NAVY	3,870
FOREST GREEN	3,640

Latch-hook, strong thread, sharp sewing needle.

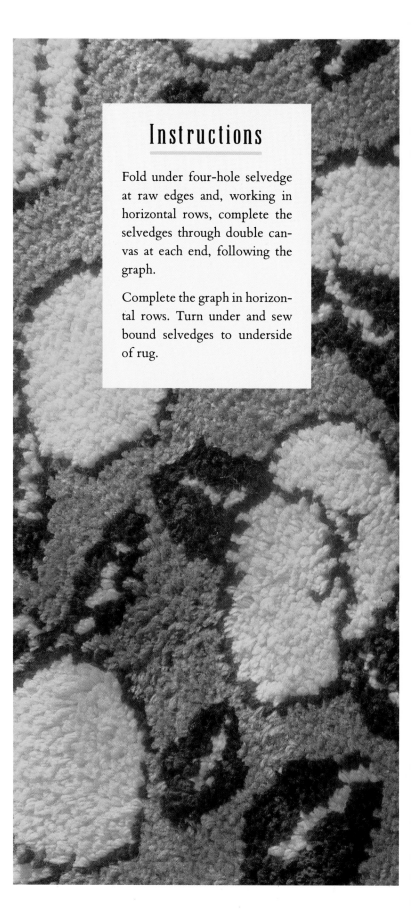

Instructions

Fold under four-hole selvedge at raw edges and, working in horizontal rows, complete the selvedges through double canvas at each end, following the graph.

Complete the graph in horizontal rows. Turn under and sew bound selvedges to underside of rug.

a SUNSHINE

b SKY BLUE

c NAVY

d FOREST GREEN

BLUE
STENCILS

Inspired by Delft pottery, this floral stencil design is easily worked in blue and white cross stitch to create a rug with a clear fresh pattern which will complement any blue and white colour scheme.

The publishers would like to thank Towsends Tiles for the loan of tiles for this photograph.

BLUE STENCILS

Method

Cross stitch (see p. 9).

Finished Size

69 × 102 cm (27 × 40 in) approximately.

Materials

Piece of cross-stitch canvas, 120 × 200 holes between selvedges, plus selvedge allowance.

Cross-stitch yarn in the following colours:

50g (2 oz) balls

ECRU 18

SKY BLUE 7

Cross-stitch needle, frame (optional).

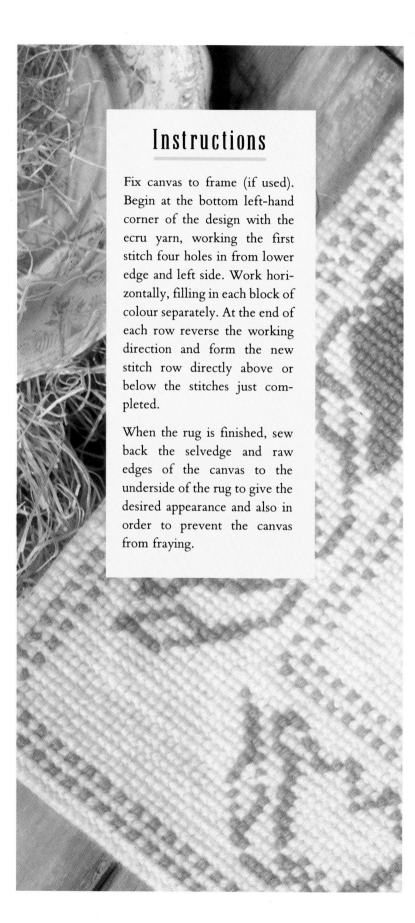

Instructions

Fix canvas to frame (if used). Begin at the bottom left-hand corner of the design with the ecru yarn, working the first stitch four holes in from lower edge and left side. Work horizontally, filling in each block of colour separately. At the end of each row reverse the working direction and form the new stitch row directly above or below the stitches just completed.

When the rug is finished, sew back the selvedge and raw edges of the canvas to the underside of the rug to give the desired appearance and also in order to prevent the canvas from fraying.

a ECRU

b SKY BLUE

TEA ROSE

This tea rose design, with
its geometric border, is
worked in delicate summer
colours.

TEA ROSE

Method

Latch-hooking.

Finished Size

77 × 137 cm (30 × 54 in) approximately.

Materials

Piece of latch-hook canvas, 99 × 181 holes between selvedges, plus selvedge allowance.

6.5-cm (2½-in) lengths of rug wool in the following colours:

	lengths
PEACH	7,880
MAUVE	4,000
BUTTER	2,710
BRAMBLE	1,910
ICE BLUE	1,290

Latch-hook, strong thread, sharp sewing needle.

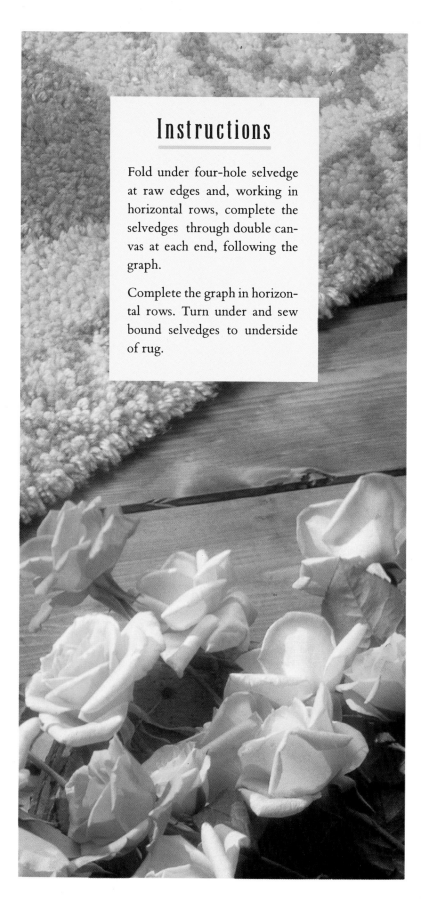

Instructions

Fold under four-hole selvedge at raw edges and, working in horizontal rows, complete the selvedges through double canvas at each end, following the graph.

Complete the graph in horizontal rows. Turn under and sew bound selvedges to underside of rug.

a PEACH
b MAUVE
c BUTTER
d BRAMBLE
e ICE BLUE

PRIMITIVE
BIRDS

This flock of birds will entertain you as you work the bold rich colours of this beautiful rug.

PRIMITIVE BIRDS

Method

Latch-hooking.

Finished Size

92 × 152 cm (36 × 60 in) approximately.

Materials

Piece of latch-hook canvas, 120 × 200 holes between selvedges, plus selvedge allowance.

6.5-cm (2½-in) lengths of rug wool in the following colours:

	lengths
BLACK	19,200
GOLD	1,180
CRIMSON	1,130
SAPPHIRE	1,000
FOREST GREEN	910
BURNT ORANGE	870

Latch-hook, strong thread, sharp sewing needle.

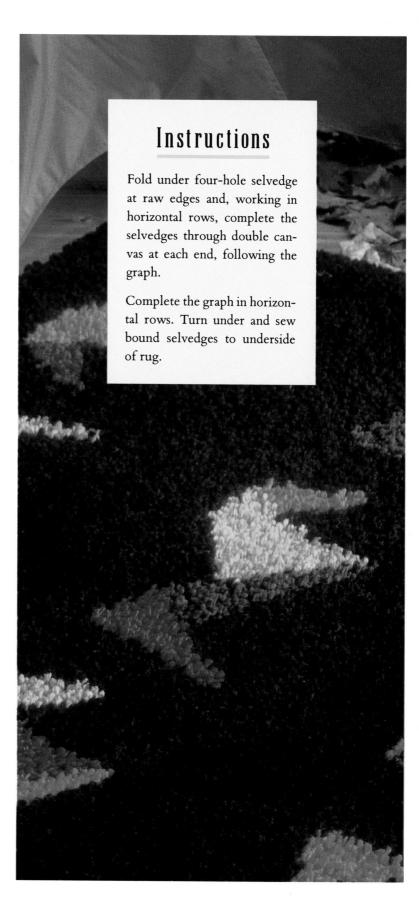

Instructions

Fold under four-hole selvedge at raw edges and, working in horizontal rows, complete the selvedges through double canvas at each end, following the graph.

Complete the graph in horizontal rows. Turn under and sew bound selvedges to underside of rug.

a BLACK

b GOLD

c CRIMSON

d SAPPHIRE

e FOREST GREEN

f BURNT ORANGE

CORNFIELD

Family crests have been a Japanese tradition since the eleventh century when they decorated the costumes and carriages of courtiers. This particular crest is worked in ecru and black to give a classic yet simple design.

CORNFIELD

Method

Latch-hooking.

Finished Size

115 × 115 cm (45 × 45 in) approximately; circular.

Materials

Piece of latch-hook canvas, 150 × 150 holes between selvedges, plus selvedge allowance.

6.5-cm (2½-in) lengths of rug wool in the following colours:

	lengths
BLACK	10,080
ECRU	7,720

Latch-hook, strong thread, sharp sewing needle, binding tape.

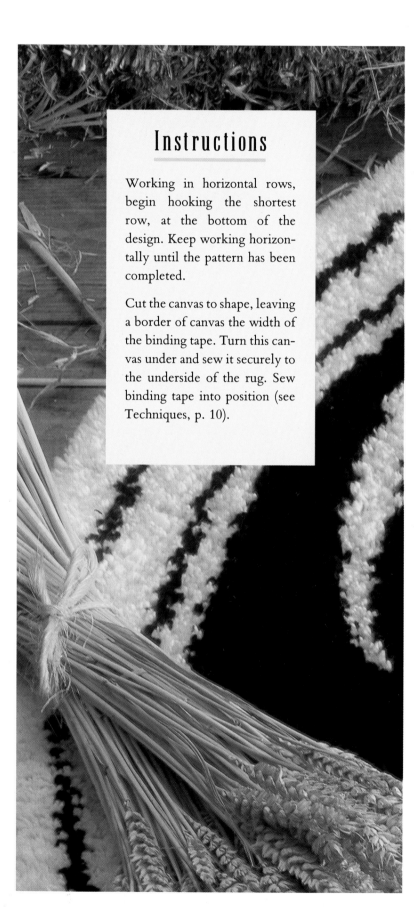

Instructions

Working in horizontal rows, begin hooking the shortest row, at the bottom of the design. Keep working horizontally until the pattern has been completed.

Cut the canvas to shape, leaving a border of canvas the width of the binding tape. Turn this canvas under and sew it securely to the underside of the rug. Sew binding tape into position (see Techniques, p. 10).

a BLACK

b ECRU

Fine Art has always influenced designers of home decor, with modern art of the twentieth century providing an especially rich and exciting source of inspiration. Rooms could be designed around these masterpieces, or the carpets would look good as stylish wall-hangings.

NUDE

Inspired by Picasso's 'Nude Woman in a Red Armchair', painted in 1932, this bold design is worked mainly in black and white with a coloured background and details. This rug is particularly suitable for wall hanging.

The publishers would like to thank Daler-Rowney for providing artists' materials for use in the photographs in this section.

NUDE

Method

Latch-hooking.

Finished Size

69 × 102 cm (27 × 40 in) approximately.

Materials

Piece of latch-hook canvas, 89 × 132 holes between selvedges, plus selvedge allowance.

6.5-cm (2½-in) lengths of rug wool in the following colours:

	lengths
ECRU	8,510
BLACK	1,960
SKY BLUE	1,890
BRIGHT RED	25

Latch-hook, strong thread, sharp sewing needle.

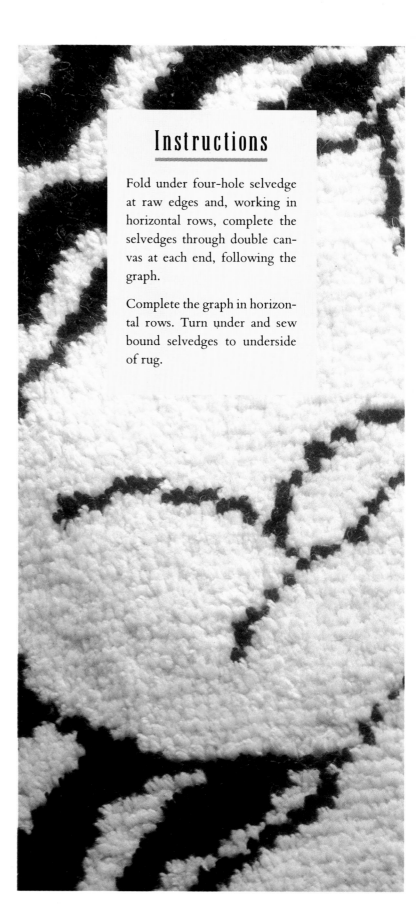

Instructions

Fold under four-hole selvedge at raw edges and, working in horizontal rows, complete the selvedges through double canvas at each end, following the graph.

Complete the graph in horizontal rows. Turn under and sew bound selvedges to underside of rug.

a ECRU
b BLACK
c SKY BLUE
d BRIGHT RED

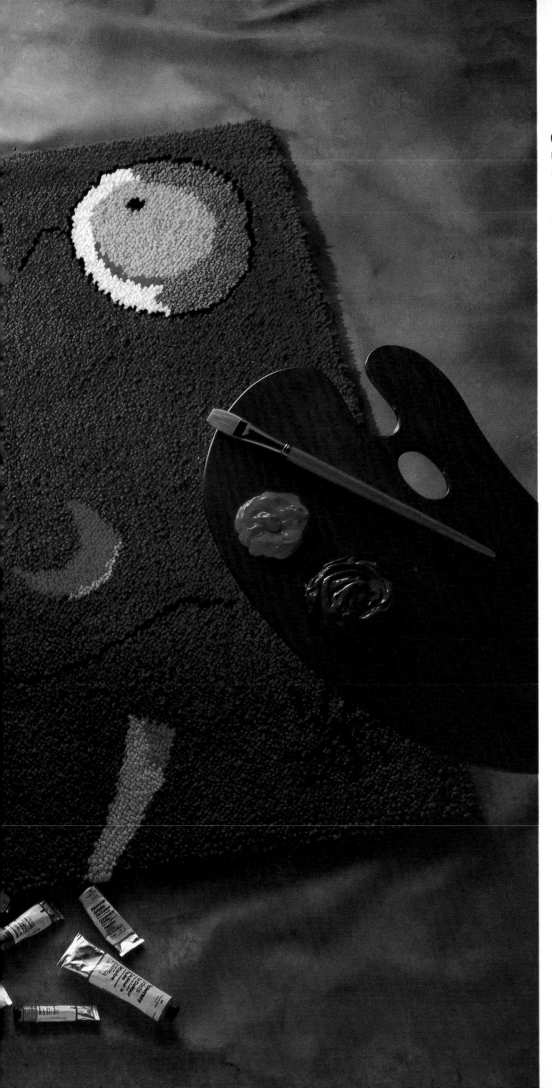

SURREALISM

Joan Miró's paintings of metamorphosed plants, humans and animals bring to life a whimsical world which echoes a more primitive time, providing a rich influence for contemporary rug designs.

SURREALISM

Method

Latch-hooking.

Finished Size

115 × 152 cm (45 × 60 in) approximately.

Materials

Piece of latch-hook canvas, 150 × 200 holes between selvedges, plus selvedge allowance.

6.5-cm (2½-in) lengths of rug wool in the following colours:

	lengths
AZURE	25,830
BRIGHT RED	1,320
SUNSHINE	1,080
BLACK	900
SAGE	525
WHITE	320

Latch-hook, strong thread, sharp sewing needle.

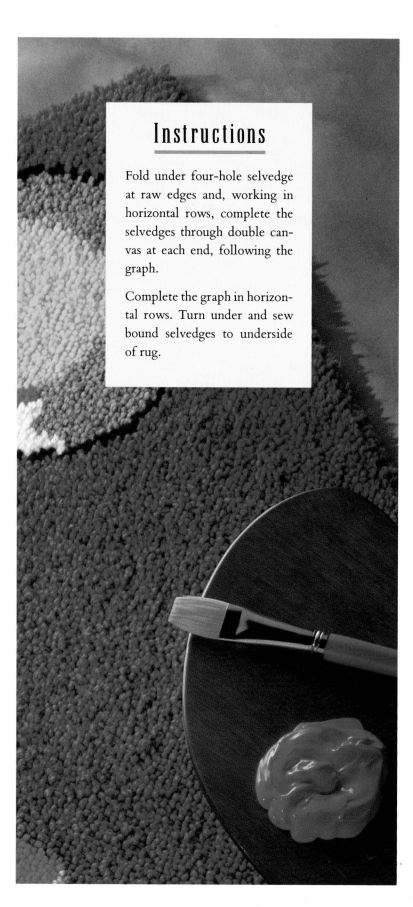

Instructions

Fold under four-hole selvedge at raw edges and, working in horizontal rows, complete the selvedges through double canvas at each end, following the graph.

Complete the graph in horizontal rows. Turn under and sew bound selvedges to underside of rug.

a AZURE   b BRIGHT RED   c SUNSHINE   d BLACK   e SAGE   f WHITE

AVANT-GARDE

Avant-garde was a name given to the leaders of a new artistic movement before the Russian Revolution. With its roots in Cubism, it expressed the energy and vitality of the time. This rug design was inspired by the work of one of these artists, Klium (1873–1942).

AVANT-GARDE

Method

Latch-hooking.

Finished Size

152 × 178 cm (60 × 70 in) approximately.

Materials

Piece of latch-hook canvas, 198 × 236 holes between selvedges, plus selvedge allowance.

6.5-cm (2½-in) lengths of rug wool in the following colours:

	lengths
SILVER	30,530
BRIGHT RED	10,560
COPPER	4,200
RICH BROWN	2,130
ECRU	1,450
BLACK	620
AZURE	190

Latch-hook, strong thread, sharp sewing needle.

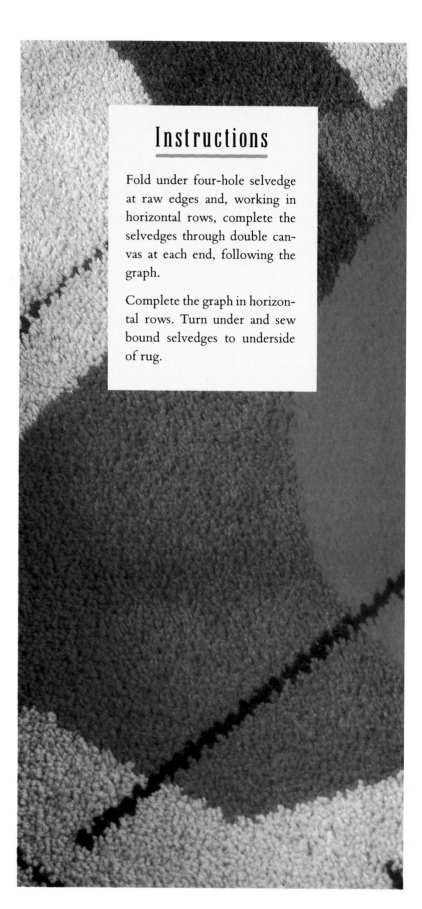

Instructions

Fold under four-hole selvedge at raw edges and, working in horizontal rows, complete the selvedges through double canvas at each end, following the graph.

Complete the graph in horizontal rows. Turn under and sew bound selvedges to underside of rug.

a SILVER   d RICH BROWN   g AZURE

b BRIGHT RED   e ECRU

c COPPER   f BLACK

ABSTRACT

One of the most important influences of twentieth-century abstract painting was Wassily Kandinsky, who was one of the first to explore the spiritual world with non-realistic art, breaking away from the confines of tradition. This rug design was inspired by Kandinsky's abstract work.

ABSTRACT

Method

Latch-hooking.

Finished Size

152 × 213 cm (60 × 84 in) approximately.

Materials

Piece of latch-hook canvas, 198 × 281 holes between selvedges, plus selvedge allowance.

6.5-cm (2½-in) lengths of rug wool in the following colours:

	lengths
NAVY	47,700
ECRU	5,870
BRIGHT RED	1,360
GOLD	1,020
AZURE	430
APPLE	390
SAPPHIRE	260
MUSHROOM	210
STONE	100

Latch-hook, strong thread, sharp sewing needle.

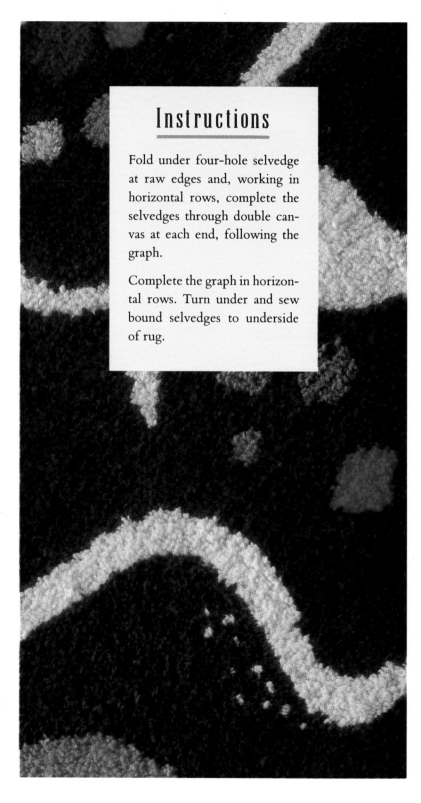

Instructions

Fold under four-hole selvedge at raw edges and, working in horizontal rows, complete the selvedges through double canvas at each end, following the graph.

Complete the graph in horizontal rows. Turn under and sew bound selvedges to underside of rug.

a NAVY	d GOLD	g SAPPHIRE
b ECRU	e AZURE	h MUSHROOM
c BRIGHT RED	f APPLE	i STONE

CONSTRUC-
TIVISM

*Constructivism was a
Russian art movement,
originating in Moscow just
after World War I, which
emphasized the explora-
tion of space. It was an
abstract movement which
had a considerable influ-
ence on architecture and
decoration. Later,
Mondrian took the explo-
ration of space further and
in his paintings he
explored equality and bal-
ance using bold line and
primary colours.*

CONSTRUCTIVISM

Method

Latch-hooking.

Finished Size

115 × 115 cm (45 × 45 in) approximately.

Materials

Piece of latch-hook canvas, 150 × 150 holes between selvedges, plus selvedge allowance.

6.5-cm (2½-in) lengths of rug wool in the following colours:

	lengths
ECRU	12,130
SILVER	3,340
BLACK	3,230
BRIGHT RED	2,880
SAPPHIRE	1,710
SUNSHINE	590

Latch-hook, strong thread, sharp sewing needle.

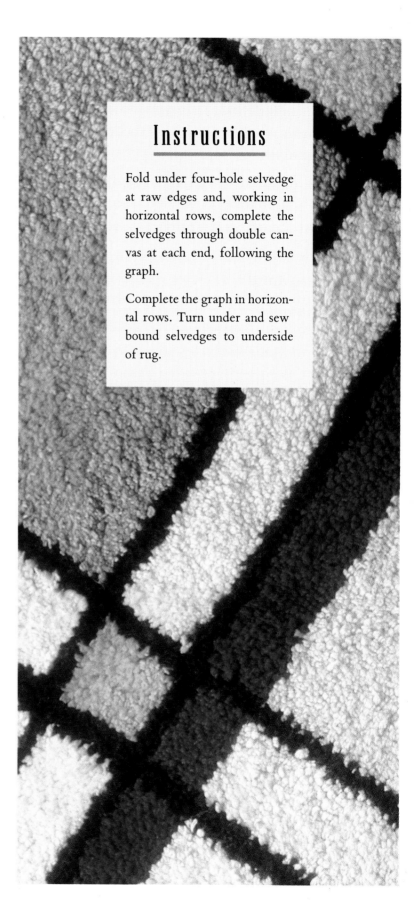

Instructions

Fold under four-hole selvedge at raw edges and, working in horizontal rows, complete the selvedges through double canvas at each end, following the graph.

Complete the graph in horizontal rows. Turn under and sew bound selvedges to underside of rug.

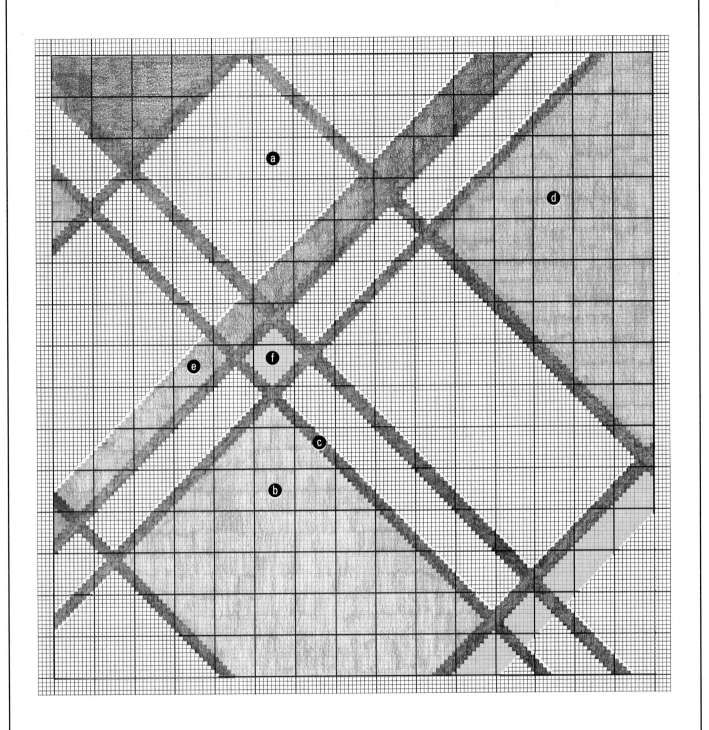

a ECRU
b SILVER
c BLACK
d BRIGHT RED
e SAPPHIRE
f SUNSHINE

These exciting contemporary designs, worked in cross stitch and latch-hooking, will complement every modern interior.

CUPID

Create a charming nursery rug with this lovely pastel cross-stitch design. Any child's name can be worked into Cupid's banner, using the alphabet provided, to make a personalized rug.

CUPID

Method

Cross stitch (see p. 9).

Finished Size

92 × 152 cm (36 × 60 in) approximately.

Materials

Piece of cross-stitch canvas, 179 × 300 holes between selvedges, plus selvedge allowance.

Cross-stitch yarn in the following colours:

	50 g (2 oz) balls
CREAM	17
SILVER BLUE	17
BABY PINK	8
GREY BLUE	3
BLUE	1
APRICOT	1
BUTTER YELLOW	1

Cross-stitch needle, frame (optional).

Instructions

Fix canvas to frame (if used). Begin at the bottom left-hand corner of the design with cream yarn, working the first stitch four holes in from lower edge and left side. Work horizontally, filling in each block of colour separately. At the end of each row reverse the working direction and form the new stitch row directly above or below the stitches you have just completed.

When the rug is finished, sew back the selvedge and raw edges of the canvas to the underside of the rug to give the desired appearance and also in order to prevent the canvas from fraying.

LETTERING

To add a child's name to Cupid's banner, first write out the name and find the middle letter. If, as in Sophie, there is no middle letter then count the space in between 'p' and 'h' as your centre. Using graph paper mark out the shape of the banner leaving out the name. Then, with the alphabet chart as your guide, mark the child's name by placing the centre letter in the centre of the banner, making sure that there is equal space between the top and bottom of the chart.

The letters should be evenly spaced and where the banner curves the letters should be moved up accordingly. If there are a lot of letters in your chosen name they may have to be reduced slightly in size in order to fit into the banner. Work in pencil first and do make sure that the letters are all the same size. When you are happy with your chart, you can work directly from it on to the rug, using each graph square for one cross stitch.

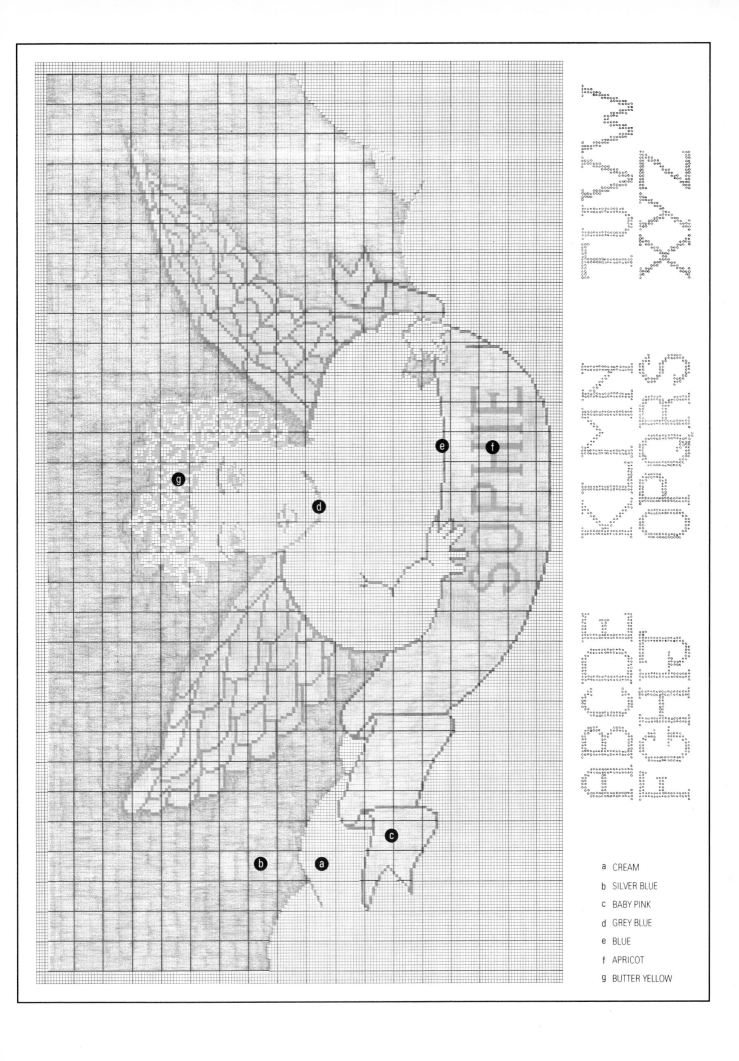

a CREAM

b SILVER BLUE

c BABY PINK

d GREY BLUE

e BLUE

f APRICOT

g BUTTER YELLOW

POPEYE

Popeye, the one-eyed, spinach-eating sailor, has been a favourite for generations. He is honest and loyal, upholds justice and is called on to trample monsters and meanies. He also looks great on this rug, a fun addition to any child's room.

POPEYE

Method

Latch-hooking.

Finished Size

92 × 92 cm (36 × 36 in) approximately.

Materials

Piece of latch-hook canvas, 120 × 120 holes between selvedges, plus selvedge allowance.

6.5-cm (2½-in) lengths of rug wool in the following colours:

	lengths
ECRU	7,240
SKY BLUE	2,480
BLACK	1,890
PEACH	1,760
CRIMSON	650
SILVER	210
SUNSHINE	200
GRASS GREEN	160
FOREST GREEN	85
COPPER	80

Latch-hook, strong thread, sharp sewing needle.

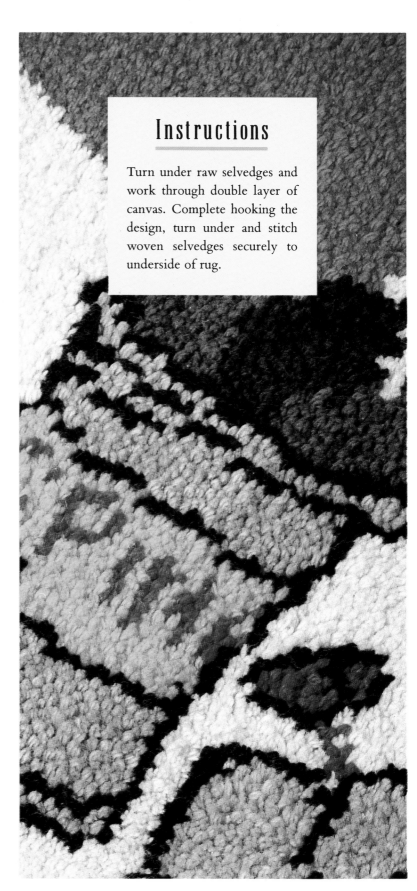

Instructions

Turn under raw selvedges and work through double layer of canvas. Complete hooking the design, turn under and stitch woven selvedges securely to underside of rug.

© *King Features Syndicates Inc.*, 1989

a	ECRU	f SILVER
b	SKY BLUE	g SUNSHINE
c	BLACK	h GRASS GREEN
d	PEACH	i FOREST GREEN
e	CRIMSON	j COPPER

HIGH
SOCIETY

A contemporary geometric pattern influenced by the Jazz Age designs of Paris in the 1920s.

HIGH SOCIETY

Method

Latch-hooking.

Finished Size

152 × 213 cm (60 × 84 in) approximately.

Materials

Piece of latch-hook canvas, 198 × 281 holes between selvedges, plus selvedge allowance.

6.5-cm (2½-in) lengths of rug wool in the following colours:

	lengths
ECRU	38,115
AZURE	4,740
NAVY	4,150
FUCHSIA	3,610
CAMEL	1,740
SUNSHINE	570

Latch-hook, strong thread, sharp sewing needle.

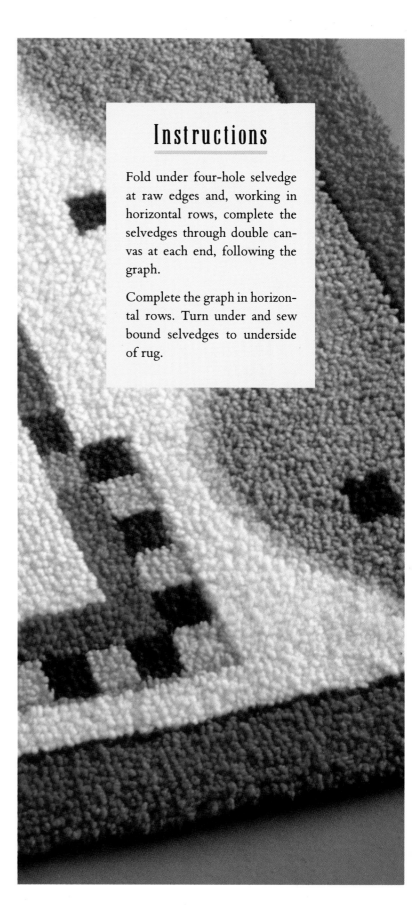

Instructions

Fold under four-hole selvedge at raw edges and, working in horizontal rows, complete the selvedges through double canvas at each end, following the graph.

Complete the graph in horizontal rows. Turn under and sew bound selvedges to underside of rug.

a ECRU   c NAVY   e CAMEL

b AZURE   d FUCHSIA   f SUNSHINE

CARIBBEAN

This attractive rug with its abstract pattern of fruit and palm leaves worked in bright primary colours will bring sunshine into any room in the house.

CARIBBEAN

Method

Latch-hooking.

Finished Size

152 × 152 cm (60 × 60 in) approximately; circular.

Materials

Piece of latch-hook canvas, 198 × 198 holes between selvedges, plus selvedge allowance.

6.5-cm (2½-in) lengths of rug wool in the following colours:

	lengths
BRIGHT RED	15,440
ECRU	7,640
SUNSHINE	2,390
FOREST GREEN	1,760
FUCHSIA	970
AZURE	760
SAPPHIRE	680
MAUVE	310
BLACK	260
BRAMBLE	220
BURNT ORANGE	160

Latch-hook, strong thread, sharp sewing needle, binding tape.

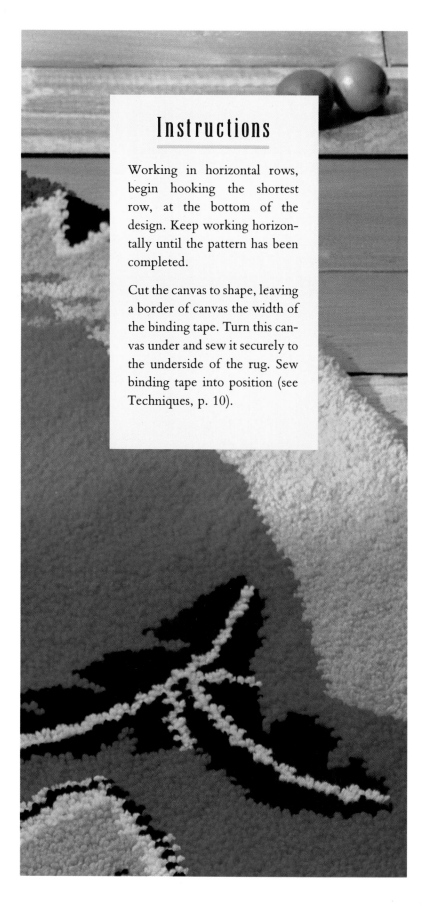

Instructions

Working in horizontal rows, begin hooking the shortest row, at the bottom of the design. Keep working horizontally until the pattern has been completed.

Cut the canvas to shape, leaving a border of canvas the width of the binding tape. Turn this canvas under and sew it securely to the underside of the rug. Sew binding tape into position (see Techniques, p. 10).

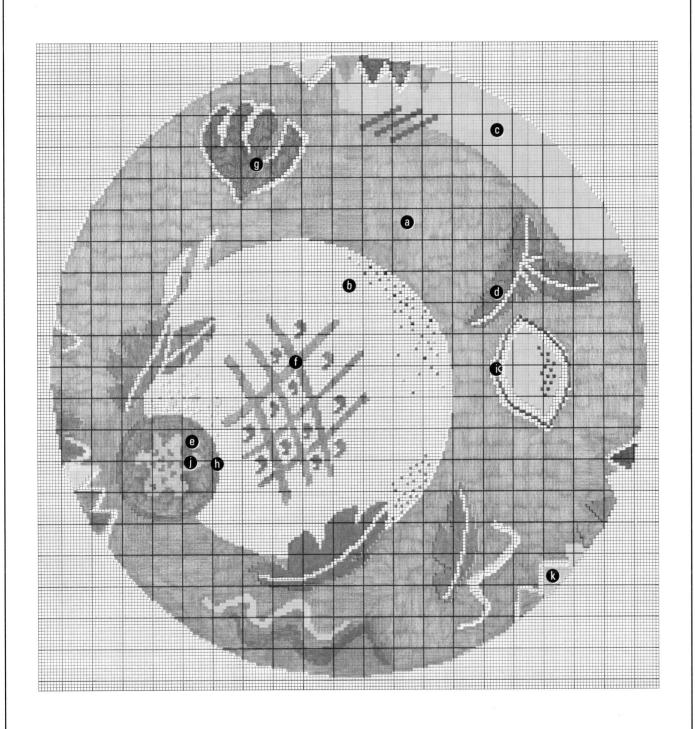

a BRIGHT RED   g SAPPHIRE

b ECRU   h MAUVE

c SUNSHINE   i BLACK

d FOREST GREEN   j BRAMBLE

e FUCHSIA   k BURNT ORANGE

f AZURE

HERALDIC
PATCHWORK

The idea behind this rug is versatility, and the final position and combination of all the designs is left to you. Each heraldic square is worked individually, enabling you to build up a rug to the shape and size you require. Any two squares joined together will make attractive cushions, and the individual pieces are small enough to be worked on your lap.

HERALDIC PATCHWORK

Method

Latch-hooking.

Finished Size

166 × 105 cm (65½ × 41 in) approximately.

Materials

To make complete rug as shown:

12 squares of latch-hook canvas, 43 × 43 holes between selvedges, plus selvedge allowance.

1 rectangle of latch-hook canvas for bottom panel, 32 × 129 holes between selvedges, plus selvedge allowance.

6.5-cm (2½-in) lengths of rug wool in the following colours:

	lengths
SAPPHIRE	8,970
WHITE	4,540
BRIGHT RED	3,870
GOLD	2,560
GRASS	1,480
NAVY	1,130
AQUA	950
BLACK	620
BEIGE	530
RICH BROWN	450

NOTE: All numbers in the boxes below refer to 6.5-cm (2½-in) lengths of rug wool.

Castle
Aqua 690
Sapphire 460
Beige 270
Bright red 180
Grass 100

Squares
(sapphire/white)
Sapphire 1,060
White 640

Crowns
White 690
Sapphire 460
Beige 260
Gold 200
Grass 90

Green/Gold Stripes
Grass 700
Gold 530
Sapphire 460

Fleur-de-lys
Bright red 1,020
Sapphire 460
Gold 210

Double Cross
White 660
Sapphire 460
Bright red 450
Black 130

Eagle
Gold 610
Sapphire 460
Rich brown 450
Bright red 100
White 70

Squares (navy/red)
Bright red 640
Navy 600
Sapphire 460

Banner
White 520
Sapphire 460
Gold 440
Bright red 250

Rose
Gold 510
Sapphire 460
Aqua 260
Bright red 230
Black 110
Grass 90
White 30

Blue Stripes
White 700
Navy 530
Sapphire 460

Cross
Bright red 680
White 540
Sapphire 460

Roses Border
Sapphire 2,190
White 690
Grass 500
Black 380
Bright red 320
Gold 60

For Joining: Sapphire 660

Latch-hook, strong thread, sharp sewing needle, binding tape.

Instructions

Allowing a <u>four-hole</u> selvedge all around <u>each</u> design, begin hooking individual squares (working in horizontal rows and starting at the lower right edge), until all the designs have been completed. Make sure you hook each square in the same direction to ensure the pile remains the same throughout.

Select the first two squares and place these side by side with the left-hand vertical selvedge of square 2 placed directly on top of the right-hand selvedge of square 1, one hole in on both edges. Using Sapphire rug wool, hook through the double thickness for two holes in a vertical line, thus joining the two squares. Trim any evident excess from square 2. Place square 3 next to square 2 and repeat process.

Select your second row of three squares and repeat as above. Repeat again for the third and fourth rows of squares.

When all the vertical joins have been completed, place the first and second rows of squares in position. Place the two rows face together so the bottom right-hand corner of square 6 is directly over the top right-hand corner of square 3. With a sharp needle and strong sewing thread join the two rows by firmly stitching through the last worked holes of the bottom of the first row of squares and the top of the second row of squares.

Repeat this process for the next two rows of squares, and again for the bottom panel.

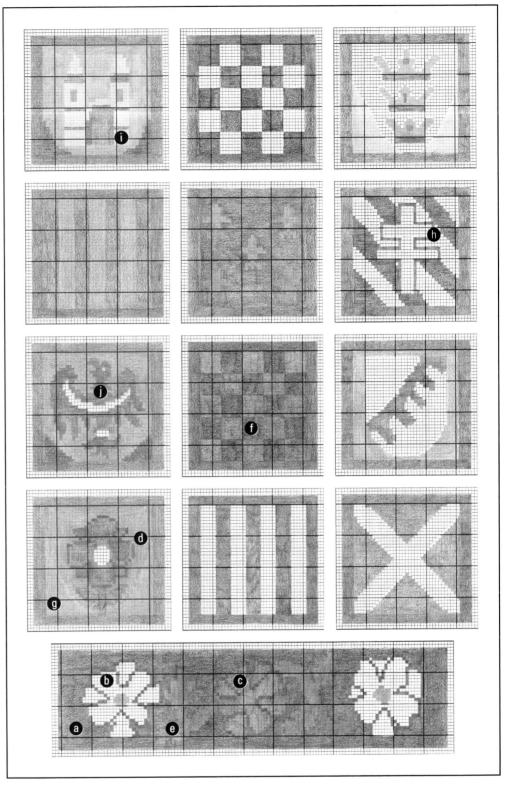

When all the pieces have been joined, stitch all the raw vertical selvedges firmly back to the underside of the rug. Turn under and stitch down all the bottom panel selvedges and finish by securely stitching strips of binding tape over all horizontal and vertical seams (see Techniques, p. 10).

a	SAPPHIRE	f NAVY
b	WHITE	g AQUA
c	BRIGHT RED	h BLACK
d	GOLD	i BEIGE
e	GRASS	j RICH BROWN

Rugs in excitingly different shapes are featured in this section. Rugs do not have to be simply square, rectangular or round, but can come in a variety of interesting forms, reflecting the theme of their design. Ideas here range from a triangular bouquet of flowers to a life-sized polar bearskin, and might inspire you to try designing your own unusual shaped rugs.

BOUQUET

This glorious bouquet of flowers, complete with bow, will brighten up any room. The triangular shape makes this rug equally attractive when used as a wall-hanging.

BOUQUET

Method

Latch-hooking.

Finished Size

152 × 152 cm (60 × 60 in) approximately.

Materials

Piece of latch-hook canvas, 198 × 200 holes between selvedges, plus selvedge allowance.

6.5-cm (2½-in) lengths of rug wool in the following colours:

	lengths
WHITE	5,630
SILVER	4,550
BRAMBLE	2,250
GRASS	1,570
APPLE	1,560
BURNT ORANGE	1,180
FUCHSIA	1,000
SAPPHIRE	870
AZURE	800
SUNSHINE	790
PALE PINK	270
CRIMSON	270
BLACK	250
POWDER BLUE	220
ECRU	90

Instructions

Lay the canvas out with the woven edges at the top and bottom. Begin hooking the design at the top right-hand corner and work downwards in horizontal rows until the design is complete.

Cut up the sloping sides of the triangle, allowing a four-hole selvedge. Cut off the top corners of the woven selvedge. Turn the side selvedges back and stitch them to the underside of the rug. Fold the top woven selvedge to the underside of the rug, placing it over the side edges so that the corners have a clean line. Sew securely into place. Repeat this process at the bottom edge.

Starting at the top right-hand corner, sew binding tape down the right side. Fold and sew across the bottom edge, then fold again and stitch securely up the left-hand side of the rug.

Latch-hook, strong thread, sharp sewing needle, binding tape.

a	WHITE	f	BURNT ORANGE	k	PALE PINK
b	SILVER	g	FUCHSIA	l	CRIMSON
c	BRAMBLE	h	SAPPHIRE	m	BLACK
d	GRASS	i	AZURE	n	POWDER BLUE
e	APPLE	j	SUNSHINE	o	ECRU

RAINCLOUD

This abstract design in stormy colours is a perfect example of the interesting effect that can be achieved by using an unusual shape.

RAINCLOUD

Method

Latch-hooking.

Finished Size

114 × 152 cm (45 × 60 in) approximately.

Materials

Piece of latch-hook canvas, 150 × 200 holes between selvedges, plus selvedge allowance.

6.5-cm (2½-in) lengths of rug wool in the following colours:

	lengths
SLATE	14,010
BLACK	6,560
WHITE	3,250
BUTTER	1,980
PALE PINK	1,250

Latch-hook, strong thread, sharp sewing needle, binding tape.

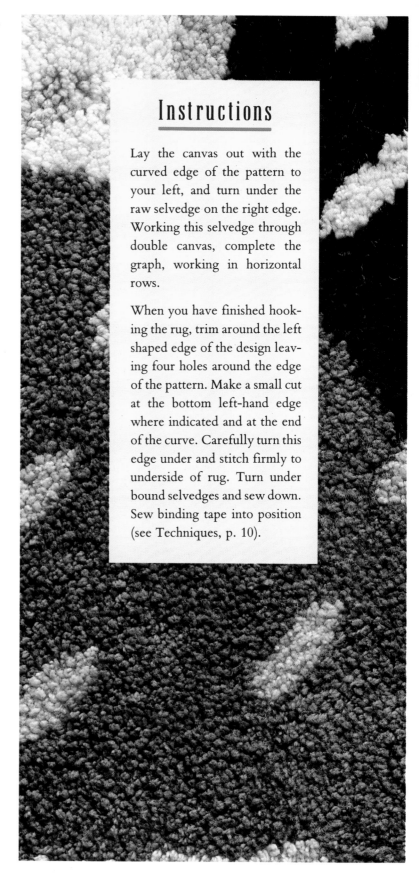

Instructions

Lay the canvas out with the curved edge of the pattern to your left, and turn under the raw selvedge on the right edge. Working this selvedge through double canvas, complete the graph, working in horizontal rows.

When you have finished hooking the rug, trim around the left shaped edge of the design leaving four holes around the edge of the pattern. Make a small cut at the bottom left-hand edge where indicated and at the end of the curve. Carefully turn this edge under and stitch firmly to underside of rug. Turn under bound selvedges and sew down. Sew binding tape into position (see Techniques, p. 10).

a SLATE
b BLACK
c WHITE
d BUTTER
e PALE PINK

POLAR
BEARSKIN

*Here is your very own
bearskin rug . . . You can
put him on the floor, drape
him over your bed, or hang
him on the wall and
impress your friends with
your hunting skills (and
no cruelty to animals is
involved).*

POLAR BEARSKIN

Method

Latch-hooking.

Finished Size

114 × 114 cm (45 × 45 in) approximately.

Materials

Piece of latch-hook canvas, 150 × 150 holes between selvedges, plus selvedge allowance.

6.5-cm (2½-in) lengths of rug wool in the following colours:

	lengths
ECRU	26,100
BLACK	70

Latch-hook, strong thread, sharp sewing needle, binding tape.

Instructions

Hook the complete design, following the chart, working in horizontal rows. Cut the canvas all around the polar bear shape leaving a four-hole selvedge. Sew the selvedge firmly to the underside of rug, cutting where necessary to ensure neat edges. Sew binding tape over all edges (see Techniques, p. 10).

Head: Fold the two top corners inwards forming a point at the centre. (The head is now cone shaped.) Overlap these two edges and stitch them firmly together.

Ears: Working each ear separately, fold them in half, wrong sides together, and tuck in raw edges. Oversew firmly all around ear. Place the flat edge of the ears down in position as shown on graph. Join the ears to the rug by oversewing firmly into position.

Ears

a ECRU

b BLACK

STAINED GLASS LANDSCAPE

Inspired by a 1930s' stained glass window design, this brightly coloured circular rug portrays a vivid summer sunset.

STAINED GLASS LANDSCAPE

Method

Latch-hooking.

Finished Size

114 × 114 cm (45 × 45 in) approximately; circular.

Materials

Piece of latch-hook canvas, 150 × 150 holes between selvedges, plus selvedge allowance.

6.5-cm (2½-in) lengths of rug wool in the following colours:

	lengths
SKY BLUE	2,740
GRASS GREEN	1,850
EMERALD	1,800
CAMEL	1,650
GOLD	1,610
MOSS GREEN	1,480
SUNSHINE	1,130
CRIMSON	1,130
PEACH	1,200
BLACK	1,000
ICE BLUE	870
FUCHSIA	830
SILVER	830
SLATE	530

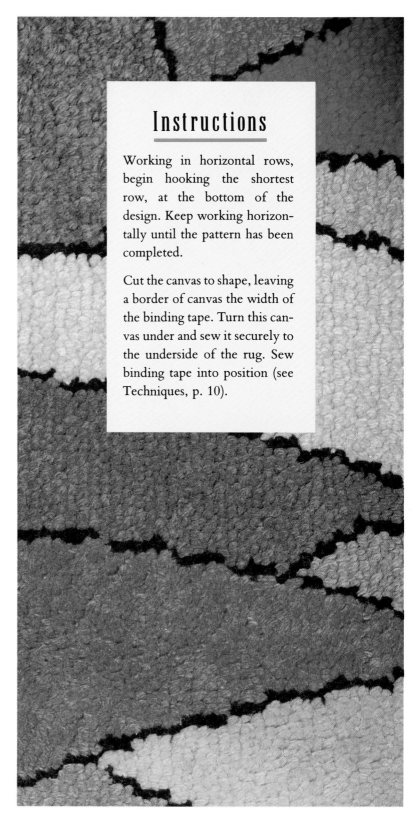

Instructions

Working in horizontal rows, begin hooking the shortest row, at the bottom of the design. Keep working horizontally until the pattern has been completed.

Cut the canvas to shape, leaving a border of canvas the width of the binding tape. Turn this canvas under and sew it securely to the underside of the rug. Sew binding tape into position (see Techniques, p. 10).

Latch-hook, strong thread, sharp sewing needle, binding tape.

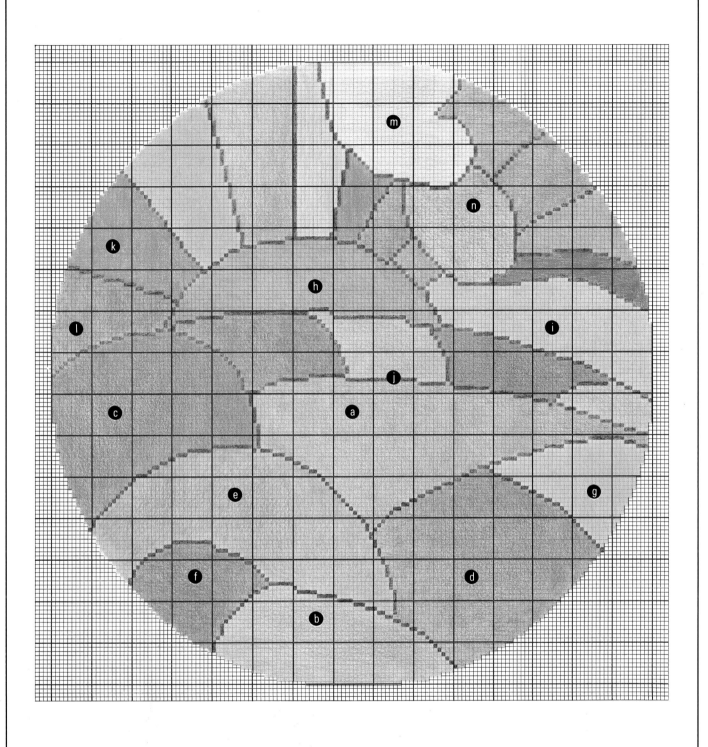

a SKY BLUE   h CRIMSON

b GRASS GREEN   i PEACH

c EMERALD   j BLACK

d CAMEL   k ICE BLUE

e GOLD   l FUCHSIA

f MOSS GREEN   m SILVER

g SUNSHINE   n SLATE

*Changing fashion is the
theme of this collection of
rugs, based on traditional
designs ranging from an
old craft pattern to a
1950s' abstract.*

FAIR ISLE

*The traditional colourful
patterns of Fair Isle knitting provide a perfect
theme for a rug design.*

FAIR ISLE

Method

Latch-hooking.

Finished Size

92 × 152 cm (36 × 60 in) approximately.

Materials

Piece of latch-hook canvas, 120 × 200 holes between selvedges, plus selvedge allowance.

6.5-cm (2½-in) lengths of rug wool in the following colours:

	lengths
TWEED	8,190
MAROON	5,250
GRASS	3,150
SKY BLUE	3,090
BURNT ORANGE	2,980
BUTTER	1,680

Latch-hook, strong thread, sharp sewing needle.

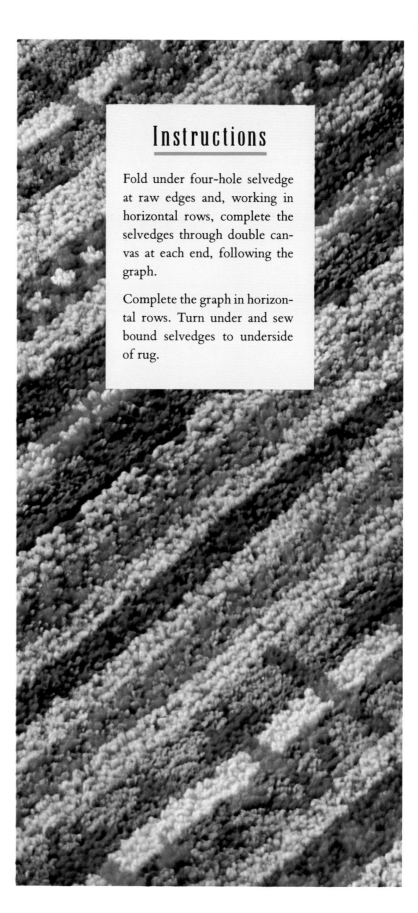

Instructions

Fold under four-hole selvedge at raw edges and, working in horizontal rows, complete the selvedges through double canvas at each end, following the graph.

Complete the graph in horizontal rows. Turn under and sew bound selvedges to underside of rug.

a TWEED

b MAROON

c GRASS

d SKY BLUE

e BURNT ORANGE

f BUTTER

ART DECO

Art Deco originally flourished in the 1920s and 1930s but is currently enjoying renewed popularity among artists and designers of home furnishings. This in turn has given rise to the high-tech style of the 1980s as in this rug design, inspired by Hollywood of the 1930s.

ART DECO

Method

Latch-hooking.

Finished Size

69 × 137 cm (27 × 54 in) approximately.

Materials

Piece of latch-hook canvas, 89 × 181 holes between selvedges, plus selvedge allowance.

6.5-cm (2½-in) lengths of rug wool in the following colours:

	lengths
BLACK	11,770
ECRU	3,720
SILVER	1,700

Latch-hook, strong thread, sharp sewing needle.

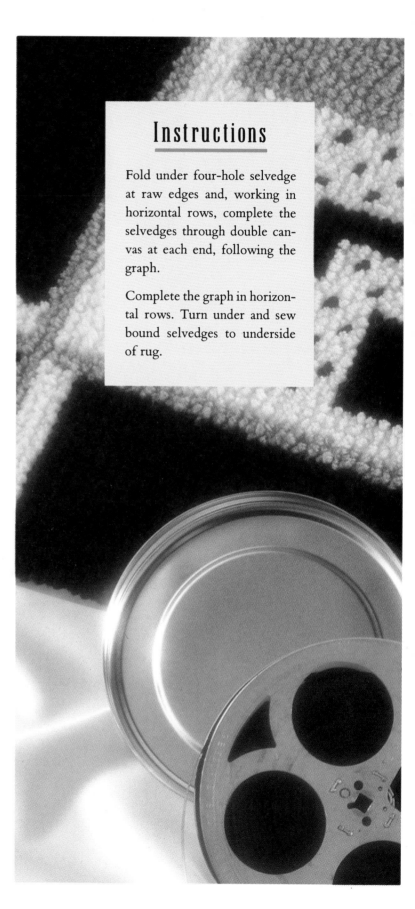

Instructions

Fold under four-hole selvedge at raw edges and, working in horizontal rows, complete the selvedges through double canvas at each end, following the graph.

Complete the graph in horizontal rows. Turn under and sew bound selvedges to underside of rug.

a BLACK
b ECRU
c SILVER

1930s'

Oriental rugs on parquet flooring were popular well into the 1930s. Then came a fashion for modern designs that complemented the tubular steel and pale wood furniture of the more commercial manufacturers. By the end of the decade the fashion had changed to linoleum with rugs of abstract design, essential in every stylish home.

1930s'

Method

Latch-hooking.

Finished Size

92 × 152 cm (36 × 60 in) approximately.

Materials

Piece of latch-hook canvas, 120 × 200 holes between selvedges, plus selvedge allowance.

6.5-cm (2½-in) lengths of rug wool in the following colours:

	lengths
BEIGE	7,580
RICH BROWN	5,570
CAMEL	3,910
JADE	3,850
CLARET	1,560
GINGER	880
GOLD	560
BURNT ORANGE	360

Latch-hook, strong thread, sharp sewing needle.

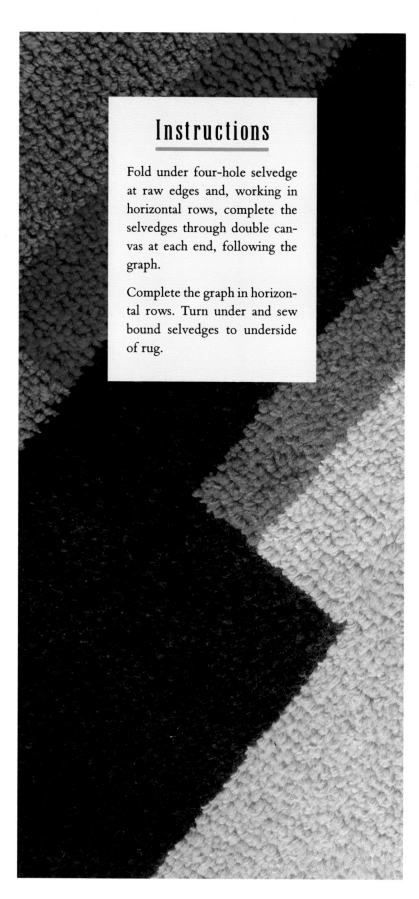

Instructions

Fold under four-hole selvedge at raw edges and, working in horizontal rows, complete the selvedges through double canvas at each end, following the graph.

Complete the graph in horizontal rows. Turn under and sew bound selvedges to underside of rug.

a BEIGE

b RICH BROWN

c CAMEL

d JADE

e CLARET

f GINGER

g GOLD

h BURNT ORANGE

1950s'
COLLAGE

In the 1950s the fashion-
able word for interior
design was 'contemporary'.
One of the major influ-
ences on 'contemporary'
design was the Festival of
Britain, with its futuristic
interest in science. The
view from a microscope, or
the shape of an atomic
structure inspired fabric
and wallpaper designs,
which were distinguished
by their flat pattern, often
with a motif enclosed in
an irregular shape.

1950s' COLLAGE

Method

Latch-hooking.

Finished Size

114 × 190 cm (45 × 75 in) approximately.

Materials

Piece of latch-hook canvas, 150 × 252 holes between selvedges, plus selvedge allowance.

6.5-cm (2½-in) lengths of rug wool in the following colours:

	lengths
ECRU	18,450
JADE	10,750
COPPER	3,590
GOLD	3,250
BLACK	2,030

Latch-hook, strong thread, sharp sewing needle.

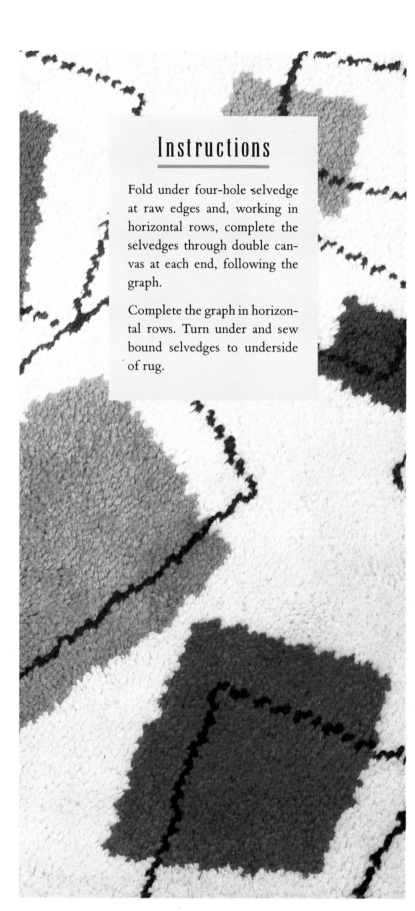

Instructions

Fold under four-hole selvedge at raw edges and, working in horizontal rows, complete the selvedges through double canvas at each end, following the graph.

Complete the graph in horizontal rows. Turn under and sew bound selvedges to underside of rug.

a ECRU
b JADE
c COPPER
d GOLD
e BLACK

USEFUL ADDRESSES

As a special service to readers of *Magic Carpets*, The Marcus Corporation offer complete kits containing hand-painted canvases and cut 100% wool yarn to match each design in the book. They also offer a making-up service for those of you who would prefer to buy the rugs readymade.

USA

Marcus Corporation
117 Dobbin Street
Brooklyn
NY 11222
New York
Tel: (718) 383-7321